Comprehensive Handwriting Practice
Modern Manuscript

Carson-Dellosa Publishing Company, Inc.

Greensboro, North Carolina

Credits

Author:
Lynette Pyne

Editors:
Ashley Anderson
Barrie Hoople

Layout Design:
Nick Greenwood

Inside Illustrations:
Bill Neville
Betsy Huffine

Cover Design:
Nick Greenwood

DN Manuscript font used with permission of Educational Fontware, Inc.

ISBN 978-1-60022-960-2

Table of Contents

Introduction

Comprehensive Handwriting Practice includes pages for practicing uppercase and lowercase letter formation and writing words and sentences about cross-curricular, age-appropriate topics. Learning and developing good handwriting skills includes mastering proper letter formation, correct proportion, and consistent spacing between letters, words, and sentences.

During each handwriting practice session:
- Instruct each student to sit upright at a desk or table with feet flat on the floor.
- Allow each student to decide which hand is most comfortable for writing.
- Be sure that each student grips the writing instrument correctly.
- Instruct each student to slightly tilt the handwriting page.
- Supervise students closely so that you can correct mistakes early without having them redo exercises.
- Keep practice sessions short, ideally 5 to 15 minutes long.
- Provide encouragement to each student.

Tips for teaching letter formation:
- Be sure students follow the arrows when practicing writing letters (Letter Practice, pages 5–17).
- Using the Letter Practice pages, have each student trace each letter using his index finger before writing.
- Students can also practice writing letters in the air, in trays of sand or cornmeal, or with finger paint.
- Teach each student how to grip a writing instrument with the thumb and index finger close to the writing tip. The remaining three fingers should rest under the index finger.
- Encourage students to visualize how the letters look. Then, they can write the letters from memory.

Tips for teaching letter proportion:
- Always use handwriting paper that has dashed middle lines.
- Explain the difference between ascenders and descenders using the mouse icons shown on pages 5–17.
- Lowercase letters with ascenders (head and body of the mouse) include *b, d, f, h, k, l,* and *t*.
- Lowercase letters without ascenders or descenders (body of the mouse) include *a, c, e, i, m, n, o, r, s, u, v, w, x,* and *z*.
- Lowercase letters with descenders (body and tail of the mouse) include *g, j, p, q,* and *y*.
- All uppercase letters have ascenders (head and body of the mouse).

When teaching spacing between words and sentences, encourage proper spacing by having students place a narrow object, such as a finger or pencil, between words and sentences.

To assemble the Tongue Twister Booklet (pages 115–128), make single-sided copies of each page. Cut off the footer from each page and cut each page in half along the cut line. Measure 3.75 inches (9.525 cm) from the cut line and trim each page. Then, arrange the booklet pages and staple the left-hand side twice vertically.

Name:

Trace and print.

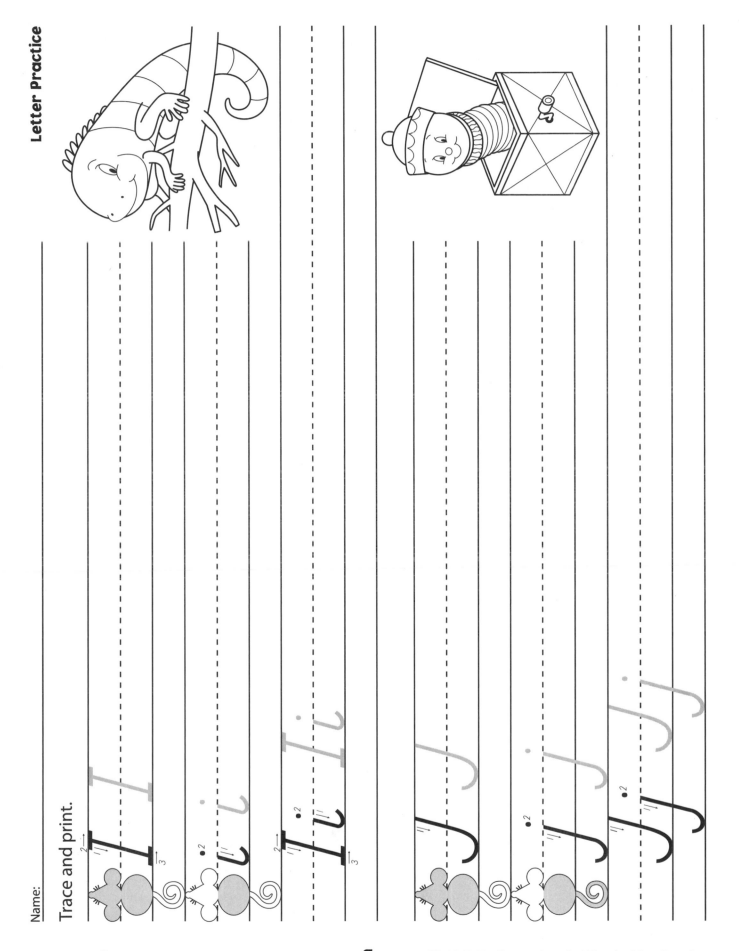

Name:

Trace and print.

Name: _____

Trace and print.

M M _____

m m _____

Mm Mm _____

N N _____

n n _____

Nn Nn _____

Name:

Trace and print.

12

Name:

Trace and print.

Qq Q Q

qq q Qq q

Qq Qq q

Rr R R

Rr r r

Rr Rr r

Name:

Trace and print.

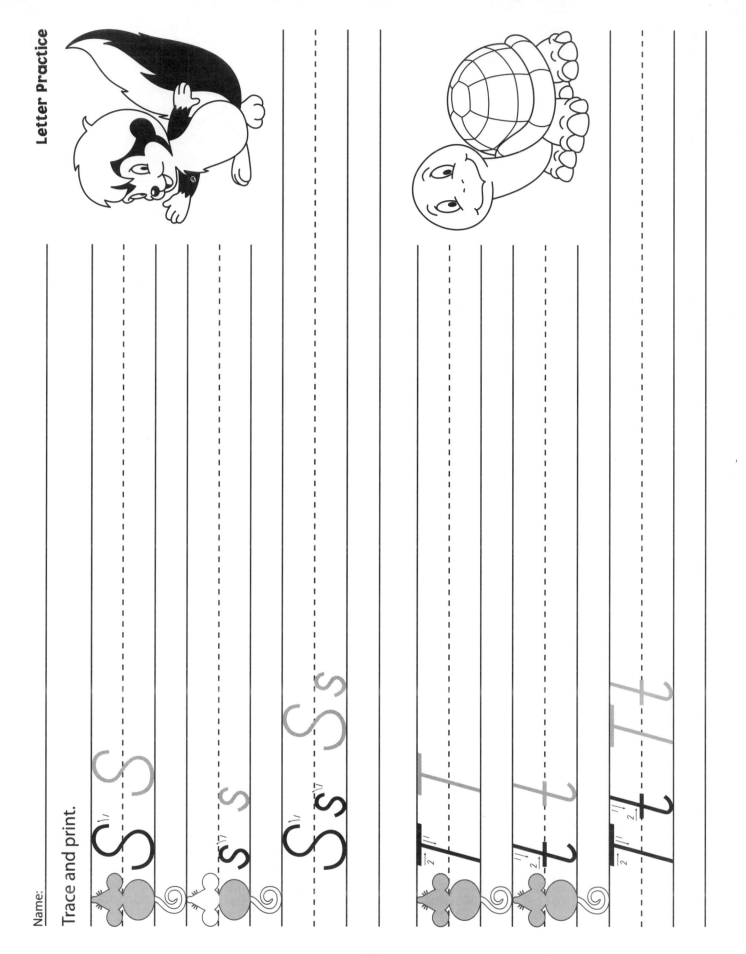

Name:

Trace and print.

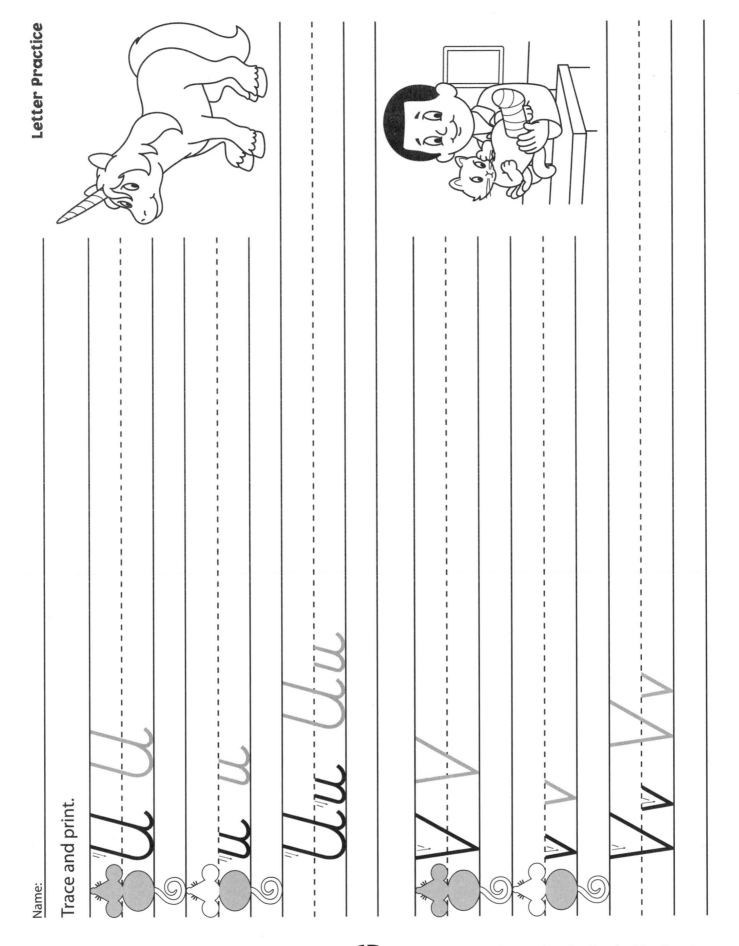

Name:

Trace and print.

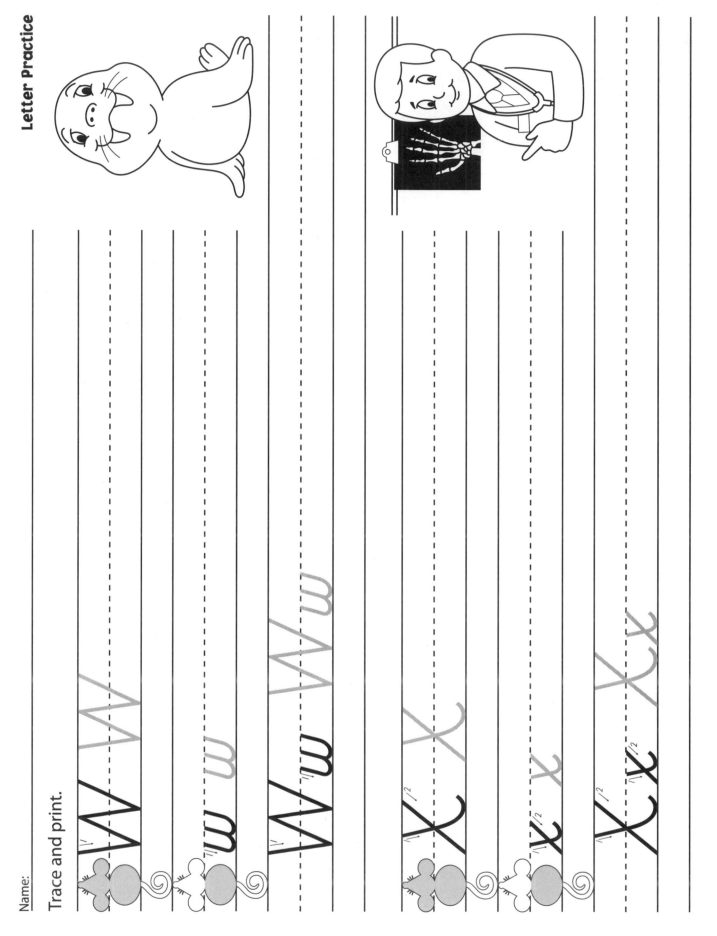

Name: _____

Trace and print.

Yy Yy Yy Yy

Zz Zz Zz Zz

Name:

Trace and print.

Aa

Andy

ate

apples

Andy and Ann ate apples.

Name: _____

Trace and print.

Bb

Barb

blew

bubbles

Barb and Bob blew bubbles.

Name:

Trace and print.

Cc

Carl

caught

caterpillar

Carl caught a caterpillar.

20

Name:

Trace and print.

Dd

Dan

dozen

doughnuts

Dan has a dozen doughnuts.

21

Name:

Trace and print.

e

Ella

eats

evening

Ella eats eggs in the evening.

Name:

Trace and print.

F f

Felix

find

frogs

Felix and Fran find frogs.

Name:

Trace and print.

Gg

Gina

green

grapes

Gina gave Gil green grapes.

24

Name:

Trace and print.

Hh

Henry

Hannah

hopped

Henry and Hannah hopped.

25

Name:

Trace and print.

I i

Ian

ice cream

igloo

Ian ate ice cream at an igloo.

26

Name:

Trace and print.

j

Jill

jump

jar

Jill and Joe jump over a jar.

Name: _____

Trace and print.

Kk

Karen

kept

kangaroo

Karen kept a kangaroo.

28

Name:

Trace and print.

L l

Luke

love

lollipops

Luke and Lola love lollipops.

Name:

Trace and print.

Mm

Meg

made

muffins

Meg and Max made muffins.

Name: _____

Trace and print.

Nn

_____

Noah

_____

new

_____

necktie

_____

Noah has a new necktie.

_____

Name:

Trace and print.

Oo

Olivia

offers

oranges

Olivia offers Oliver oranges.

32

Name:

Trace and print.

Pp

Pat

popped

popcorn

Pat and Pam popped popcorn.

33

Name:

Trace and print.

Qq

Queen

quite

quilt

Queen Kim has quite a quilt.

34

Name:

Trace and print.

Rr

Rick

rocky

road

Rick runs on a rocky road.

35

Name:

Trace and print.

Ss

Sara

sing

songs

Sara and Sam sing songs.

Name:

Trace and print.

Tt

Tt

Tim

$twinkling$

$tricycle$

$Tim\ has\ a\ twinkling\ tricycle.$

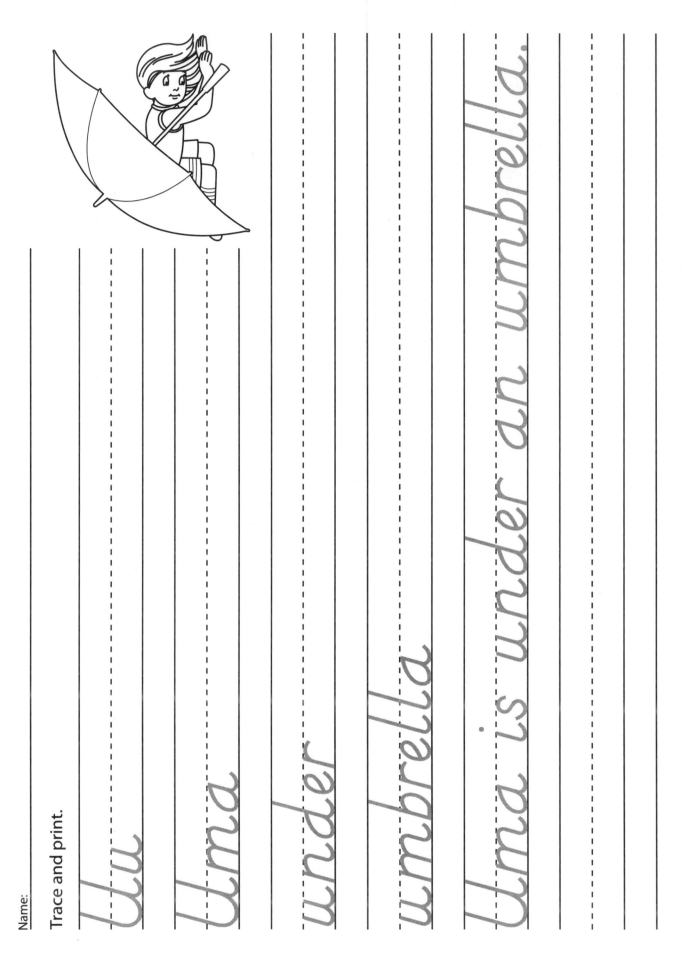

Name: _____

Trace and print.

Uu

Uma

under

umbrella

Uma is under an umbrella.

Name: _____

Trace and print.

Vv

Vance

visits

vacation

Vance visits Viv on vacation.

Name:

Trace and print.

Ww

Walt

wobbly

wagon

Walt has a wobbly wagon.

Name:

Trace and print.

Xx

Xandra

box

foxes

Xandra sees a box of foxes.

41

Name:

Trace and print.

Yy

Yasmin.

yelled

yodeled

Yasmin. yelled and yodeled.

Name:

Trace and print.

Zz

Zack

zany

zoo

Zack has a zany zoo map.

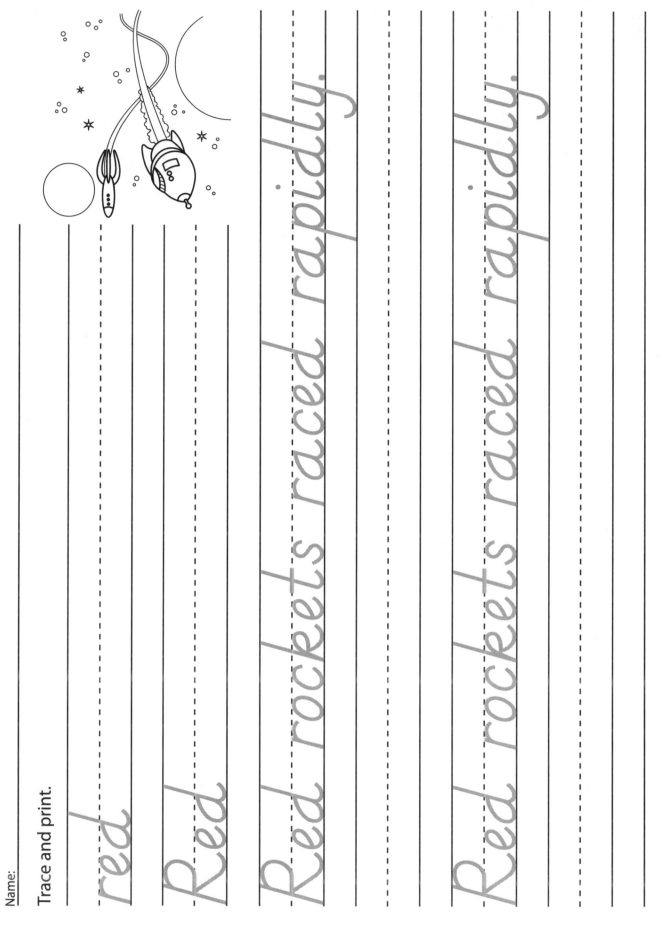

Name: _____

Trace and print.

red

Red

Red rockets raced rapidly.

Red rockets raced rapidly.

44

Name:

Trace and print.

orange

Orange

The octopus owns oranges.

The octopus owns oranges.

45

Name: _____

Trace and print.

yellow

Yellow

A yak has a yellow yo-yo.

A yak has a yellow yo-yo.

46

Name: _____

Trace and print.

green

Green

The green gorillas giggled.

The green gorillas giggled.

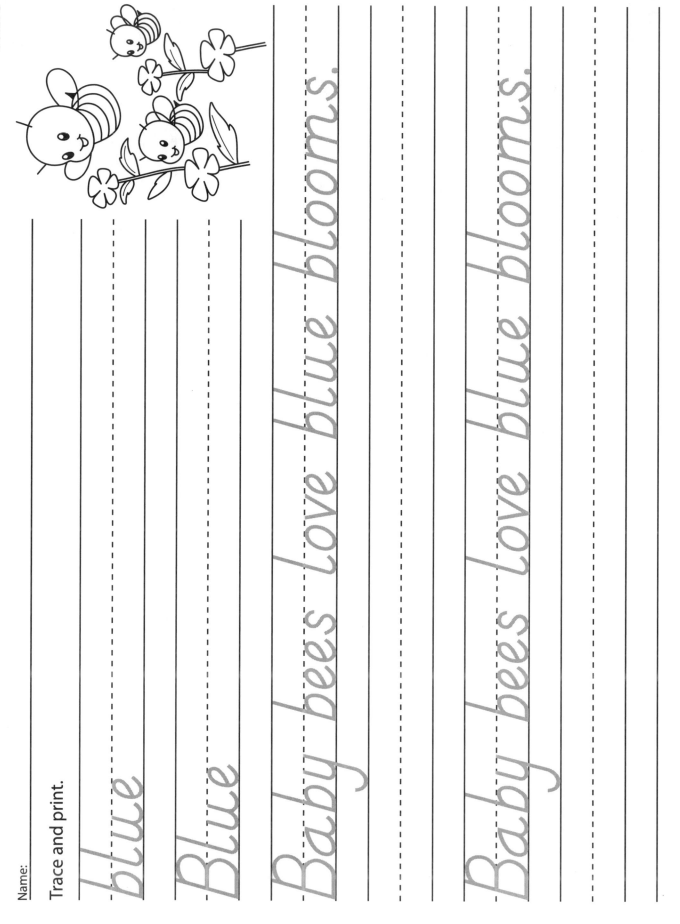

Name:

Trace and print.

blue

Blue

Baby bees love blue blooms.

Baby bees love blue blooms.

48

Name:

Trace and print.

purple

purple

Patti picks purple pansies.

Patti picks purple pansies.

49

Name: _____

Trace and print. Then, color the picture using the colors below.

red   orange   yellow

green   blue   purple

Name: _____

Trace and print.

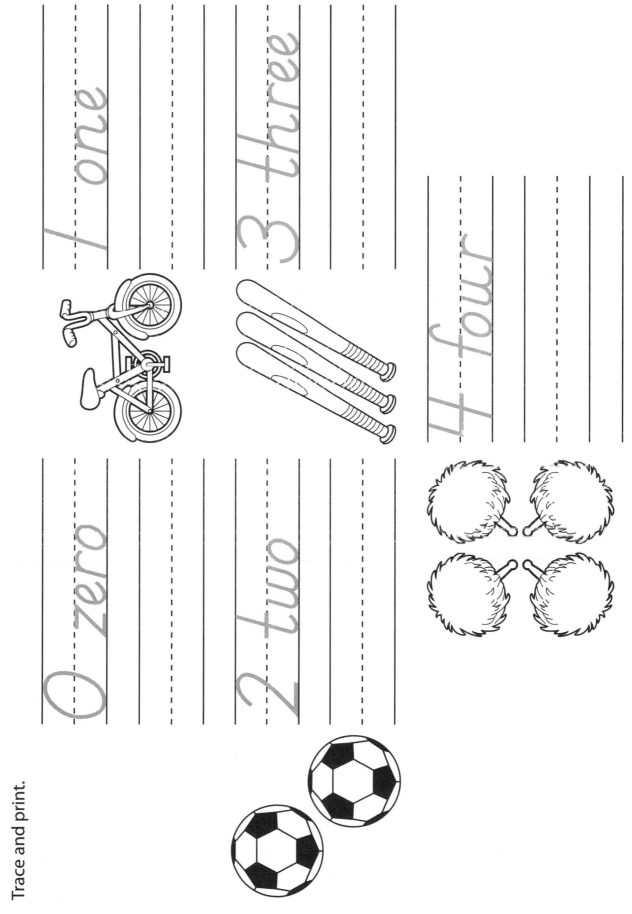

0 zero

1 one

2 two

3 three

4 four

51

Name:

Trace and print.

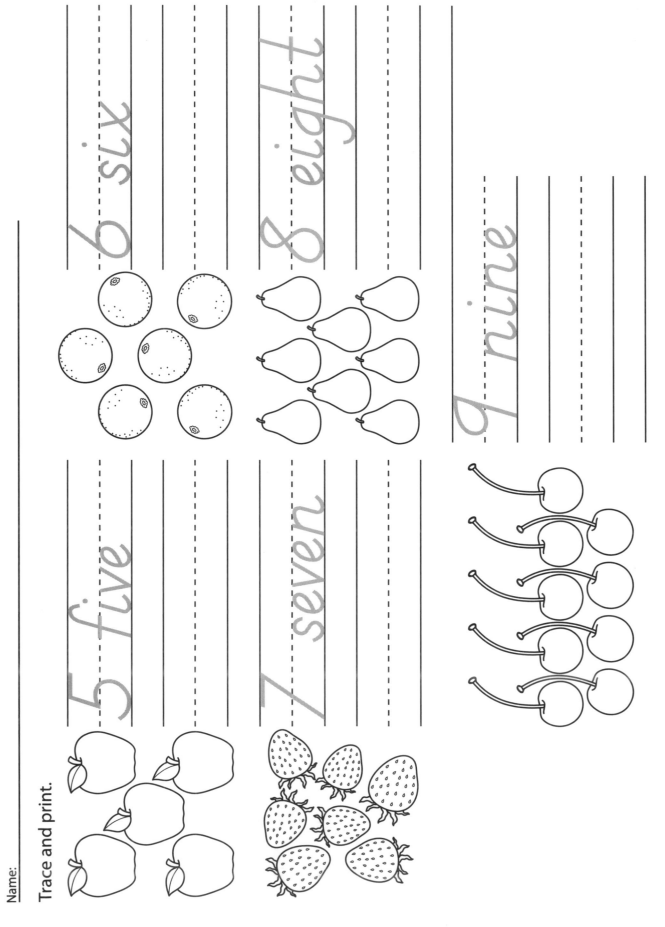

5 five

6 six

7 seven

8 eight

9 nine

Name: _____

Trace and print.

zero one two three four

_____

zero one two three four

_____

Name: _____

Trace and print.

five   six   seven   eight   nine

five   six   seven   eight   nine

54

Name:

Trace and print.

Sun.	Mon.	Tues.
1	2	3

Sunday

Sunday is the first day of

the week.

Sun.	Mon.	Tues.
1	2	3

Name:

Trace and print.

Monday

Monday is the second day

of the week.

Name: _____

Trace and print.

Tuesday

Tuesday is the third day

of the week.

	Tues.	Wed.	Thurs.
	3	4	5

Name:

Trace and print.

Wednesday

Wednesday is the fourth

day of the week.

58

Wed.	Thurs.	Fri.
4	5	6

Name:

Trace and print.

Thursday

Thursday is the fifth day

of the week.

CD-104247 • Comprehensive Handwriting Practice

Thurs.	Fri.	Sat.
5	6	7

Name:

Trace and print.

Friday

Friday is the sixth day of the week.

Thurs.	Fri.	Sat.
5	6	7

Name: _____

Trace and print.

Saturday

_____

Saturday is the seventh

_____

day of the week.

_____

Name:

Trace and print.

circle

Circles have 0 sides.

triangle

Triangles have 3 sides.

Name: _____

Trace and print.

square

Squares have 4 sides.

rectangle

Rectangles have 4 sides.

Name:

Trace and print.

trapezoid

Trapezoids have 4 sides.

oval

Ovals have 0 sides.

Name: _____

Trace and print.

pentagon

Pentagons have 5 sides.

hexagon

Hexagons have 6 sides.

Name: _____

Trace and print.

2:00

4:00

1:00

3:00

I will play outside at 2:00.

Name:

Trace and print.

6:00

8:00

5:00

7:00

I eat breakfast at 7:00.

Name:

Trace and print.

10:00

2:00

Marcus will call at 1:00.

9:00

11:00

68

Name:

Trace and print.

2:30

4:30

1:30

3:30

Recess is at 1:30 today.

Name:

Trace and print.

6:30

8:30

5:30

7:30

Dad starts dinner at 6:30.

Name:

Trace and print.

10:30

12:30

9:30

11:30

I leave for camp at 9:30.

Name:

Trace and print.

fall

chilly

apples

pumpkins

The leaves change colors.

Name: _____

Trace and print.

summer

hot

swim

pool

The sun shines brightly.

Name: _____

Trace and print.

fall

winter

spring

summer

We really enjoy them all!

Name:

Trace and print.

January

February

March

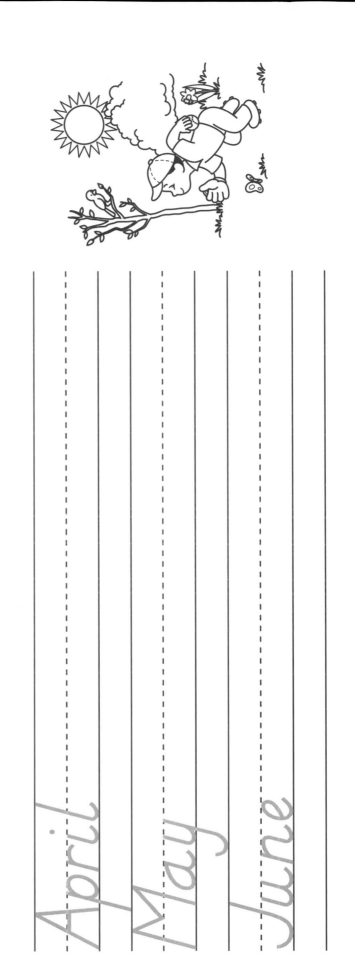

April

May

June

Name: _____

Trace and print.

July

August

September

October

November

December

Name: _____

Trace and print.

pear

house

snake

snail

bee

duck

bear

mouse

cake

nail

tree

truck

Name: _____

Trace and print.

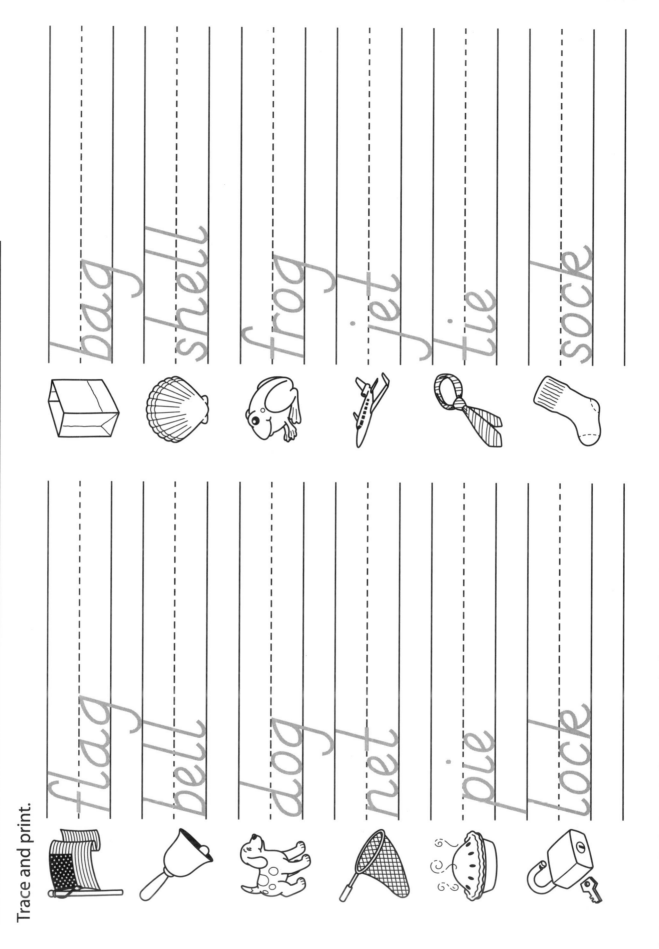

bag

shell

frog

jet

tie

sock

flag

bell

dog

net

pie

lock

Name:

Trace and print.

violin

harp

The violin and the harp are

stringed instruments.

Name:

Trace and print.

drum

cymbal

Drums and cymbals are

percussion instruments.

82

Name:

Trace and print.

saxophone

flute

The saxophone and the flute

are woodwind instruments.

Name: _____

Trace and print.

piano

organ

The piano and the organ

are keyboard instruments.

84

Name:

Trace and print.

trumpet

tuba

The trumpet and the tuba

are brass instruments.

Name:

Australia is the smallest continent.
Many interesting and unique animals
live in Australia.

Copy the sentences in your best handwriting.

Name:

An echidna looks like a porcupine.

It eats ants and termites.

The echidna curls into a ball

when it is scared.

Copy the sentences in your best handwriting.

87

Name:

A wallaby looks like a small kangaroo.

It has strong hind legs.

Wallabies have pouches to carry

their babies.

Copy the sentences in your best handwriting.

Name: _____

Koalas are not bears.

They are marsupials.

Koalas eat leaves from eucalyptus trees.

They also sleep in trees.

Copy the sentences in your best handwriting.

Name:

Tasmanian devils hunt for food at night.

They do not like to share food.

They are small but very strong!

Copy the sentences in your best handwriting.

90

Name: _____

The platypus has a bill and webbed
feet like a duck.
It has fur and a flat tail like a beaver.
It likes to swim.

Copy the sentences in your best handwriting.

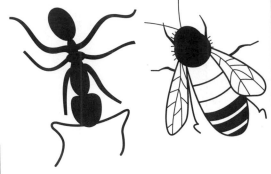

Name:

Many ants work together to
build nests and gather food.

Bees gather pollen.

Some bees make honey.

Copy the sentences in your best handwriting.

92

Name:

Crickets chirp by rubbing
their wings together.
Some people think that
ladybugs bring good luck.

Copy the sentences in your best handwriting.

Name:

Butterflies collect
nectar from flowers.
Grasshoppers have strong
back legs for jumping.

Copy the sentences in your best handwriting.

94

Name:

An invention begins when
someone has an idea.
Inventors create new
things using their ideas.

Copy the sentences in your best handwriting.

Name: _____

A boy named Tom
invented the snowboard.

It is like a skateboard without wheels.

It is used on snow.

Copy the sentences in your best handwriting.

Name: _____

The first toothbrushes were twigs
with bristles attached to the ends.
They looked like stiff paintbrushes.

Copy the sentences in your best handwriting.

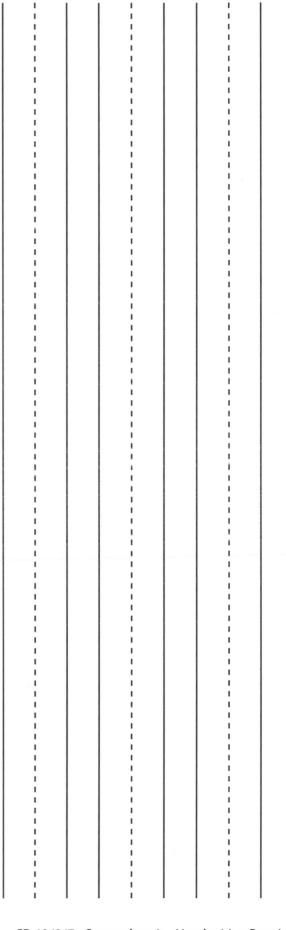

97

Name: _____

A boy named George
invented the trampoline.
He got the idea when he
saw acrobats at a circus.

Copy the sentences in your best handwriting.

98

Name: _____

The first erasers were

pieces of bread.

Today, most erasers are

made of rubber.

Copy the sentences in your best handwriting.

Name:

Community helpers
Are there in many ways.
We count on them so much
On this day and always!

Copy the poem in your best handwriting.

100

Name:

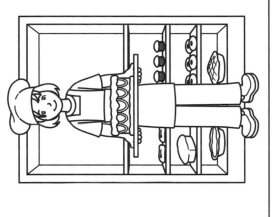

A baker is someone
We couldn't be without.
Those cookies and desserts,
We always dream about.

Copy the poem in your best handwriting.

Name:

The brave firefighters' job
Is dangerous indeed!
They protect us from fires
Wherever there's a need.

Copy the poem in your best handwriting.

102

Name:

Mail carriers help
By bringing us our mail.
They bring it to our homes;
They do it without fail.

Copy the poem in your best handwriting.

Name: _____

Librarians help you

To find that special book.

They are great helpers;

They know just where to look.

Copy the poem in your best handwriting.

Name:

If your pets are not well,

You give the vet a call.

A vet will care for them,

And all pets, big and small.

Copy the poem in your best handwriting.

Name: _____

Cooking in the kitchen

Is so much fun to do.

I'm making tasty treats

To share with all of you!

Copy the poem in your best handwriting.

106

Name:

Ants on a Log

1. Wash a piece of celery.

2. Spread peanut butter on it.

3. Add raisins on top.

Copy the recipe in your best handwriting.

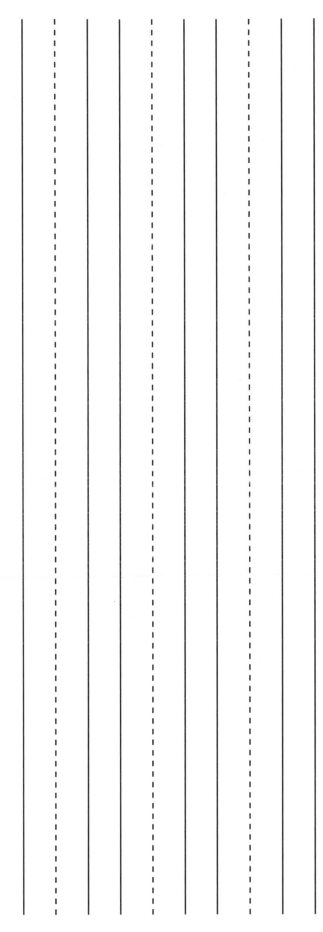

107

Name:

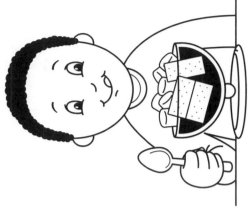

S'mores in a Bowl

1. Put graham crackers in a bowl.

2. Add chocolate pudding.

3. Add small marshmallows.

Copy the recipe in your best handwriting.

Name: _____

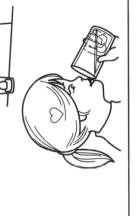

Lemonade

1. Put powdered mix in a cup.

2. Add cold water.

3. Stir and enjoy.

Copy the recipe in your best handwriting.

Name:

Casey has 2 red cars and 4 blue cars. How many cars does he have altogether?

Copy the word problem in your best handwriting. Then, solve the problem.

110

Name: _____

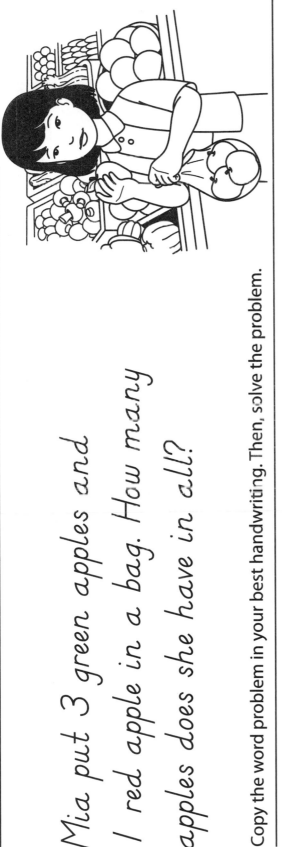

Mia put 3 green apples and 1 red apple in a bag. How many apples does she have in all?

Copy the word problem in your best handwriting. Then, solve the problem.

Name: _____

Dad put 5 hot dogs on a tray. Sam ate 2 of them. How many hot dogs are left?

Copy the word problem in your best handwriting. Then, solve the problem.

- -

Name: _____

The pet store had 6 kittens for sale. They sold 2 kittens. How many kittens are left?

Copy the word problem in your best handwriting. Then, solve the problem.

Name: _____

Carrie had a set of 8 markers. She lost 2 of them. How many markers does she have left?

Copy the word problem in your best handwriting. Then, solve the problem.

My
Tongue Twister
Booklet

by:

Name:

Aa

Angry ants argue.

CD-104247 • Comprehensive Handwriting Practice

Name:

Bb

The black bike broke.

✂

Name:

Cc

Cal ate crispy crackers.

116

Name:

Dd

A dinosaur digs deep.

Name:

Ee

Eight electric eels eat.

CD-104247 • Comprehensive Handwriting Practice

Name:

Ff

Eat frogs fly fast.

Name:

Gg

Gail grabbed grapes.

Name: _____

Hh

Hamsters hum happily.

✂ Name: _____

Ii

Iggy's igloo has icicles.

 CD-104247 • Comprehensive Handwriting Practice

Name:

Jam

Jam jars are jiggling.

Name:

Kk

King Kevin keeps kites.

Name:

Ll

Ladybugs love leaves.

Mm

Mice make music.

Name:

Nn

Nancy nibbles noodles.

Name:

Oo

Otters open oranges.

Name:

P
Pp
Pandas pick pick petunias.

Name:

Qq
Quickely quit quacking!

123

Name:

R r

Raccoons recite rhymes.

Name:

S s

Smart sharks swim.

Name:

Tt

Two toads taste tacos.

Name:

Uu

Unicorns use ukuleles.

125

Name:

Vv

Val values valentines.

Name:

Ww

William wants winter.

Name:

Xx

Dr. Rex examines X-rays.

Name:

Yy

Yaks yell and yodel.

CD-104247 • Comprehensive Handwriting Practice

Name: _____

Zz

Zany zebras zigzag.